BEVELED EDGES AND MITERED CORNERS

POEMS

BEVELED EDGES AND MITERED CORNERS

POEMS

MARY ELIZABETH LEE

BEVELED EDGES AND MITERED CORNERS
POEMS

iUniverse books may be ordered through booksellers or by contacting:

iUniverse
1663 Liberty Drive
Bloomington, IN 47403
www.iuniverse.com
1-800-Authors (1-800-288-4677)

Because of the dynamic nature of the Internet, any web addresses or links contained in this book may have changed since publication and may no longer be valid. The views expressed in this work are solely those of the author and do not necessarily reflect the views of the publisher, and the publisher hereby disclaims any responsibility for them.

Any people depicted in stock imagery provided by Thinkstock are models, and such images are being used for illustrative purposes only.
Certain stock imagery © Thinkstock.

ISBN: 978-1-4917-6849-5 (sc)
ISBN: 978-1-4917-6850-1 (e)

Library of Congress Control Number: 2015909257

Print information available on the last page.

iUniverse rev. date: 7/8/2015

ACKNOWLEDGMENTS

Thanks to the editor of *Black & Rouge Review* where the following poems first appeared:

Black & Rouge Review 1, no. 1 (Spring 2008)
    "An Urge"
    "An Open Letter to Adrienne Rich"
    "The Poet"
    "Sighting"
    "Unnatural Death"

Black & Rouge Review 2, no. 1 (Spring 2009)
    "The Gift"
    "Silence"

Black & Rouge Review 3, no. 1 (Spring 2010)
    "Life along the Hypothetical"

CONTENTS

SUNDAY DRIVE

A Sunday drive stopped on the roadside
reveals a time disappearing. As far as
I can see, encroaching green thickets of pine and oak
collar the sunbaked and weed-strewn farmland
where pines whisper to the blue horizon,
where all around no clouds preside to answer.
Once carefully furrowed and terraced,
isolated clusters of black-eyed Susans
dot the acres surrounding the old homeplace,
rising like a small butte, a faithful memory
fiercely clinging. With precious little but land,
painted in a mixture of summer's palette
of red clover, wild verbena, and goldenrod,
once tended low by grazing Herefords and Angus,
its inhabitants are land poor. Around
the blue hemisphere, above
one lone cloud from nowhere watches,
a sculptured fluff of whipped cream.
Friendly winds nudge it on its way.
Beyond the thickets, I watch it float
between the green of the trees
and the blue of the sky as a breeze
nudges me on to my afternoon destiny in the city.

HOT SUMMER SUNDAYS

Hot summer Sundays
once seemed like fun.
Past black-eyed Susans
along the state road
and beyond creeping vetch
from the farmlands
to the turn left off the highway
and two miles down the dirt road
rutted by log trucks and summer rains.
I remember another summer Sunday past
when I made this same trip,
my legs swinging, heels
thump-thumping against the car seat.
That same burning excitement
now rises inside me like acid.
From the thick, towering pines
on both sides of the road,
the fresh, sweet smell of pine straw
fills the car as it filled me
with dreams of when I was nine.
A sentry blue jay in a sweeping pass
announces our arrival
while the birds in the thickets
chatter their surprise and
an alerted squirrel scampers
across the car's path.
Turning the curve, then up the hill,
the car strains in third to climb
the red clay incline:
the old homeplace sits before me.

NATURE'S FAVORITE CHILD

Your stoic disposition I have chanced,
and your temerarious guile too,
outsmarting home owner and farmer alike,
poking your green spears through surfaces
only newly tarred—what is your purpose?
Should I not ask what I can guess?
Without invitation, without welcome
or appreciation, persistent and zealous,
you appear to turn a brown surface fertile green.
In seeds burrowed deep or on winds flown wide,
you survive, blending, mending Mother Earth's pride.
Drone weed, are you nature's favorite child?
In underground factories of moisture and earth,
under cement skies and sediment suns,
you tunnel a maze of roots to house
earthworms and friends like spies from view.
Overnight fertile worlds for the perennial belles
and the ambassadorial trees,
your odd network maze emerges.
Dedicated one, in another world coming,
man-spun, brave and scientific,
your freedom and purpose denied,
beware of gaseous powders that will
cause you to explode and die
when you dare to tunnel through to sunlight,
dare to slip between concrete squares
and spear through asphalt spread wide,
or push up between rows of towering corn
or tomatoes staked tall. Favorite child,
what is Mother Nature to do?

ASYMMETRY

I read somewhere
that nature prefers asymmetry,
and that is the long and the short
of it, as in the neck of the giraffe,
the life of the housefly,
the tail of the bobcat.
Love too is the long
and the short of it.
Seventy-five to twenty-five
percent is what's meant
to the bent backs of many—
life and love in one, ten,
fifty, or a hundred increments
daily, weekly, monthly, yearly,
in bits and pieces of newsprint,
pink pay slips, utility readings,
birthday and anniversary greetings.
But what's this? Do I digress?
On the right or the left of the matter,
where right is the preferred,
nature prefers the left-handed:
parrots prefer picking up things with the left foot,
preying toads attack from the left,
zebra fish view the familiar with their left eye,
the stealth neutrino appears only when left-handed.
So it is, in the curl of the ram's horn,
the improbable flight of the bumblebee,
the amino acids of life and wine,
the unique to transform the genes
in the inherent pattern of scheme.
In the long and the short of it,
on the right or the left
of the scheme of things—
rest easy, Pelagius.
Nature still knows best.

STANDOFF

Cool hangs from the warm sky
in the standoff between Fading
Summer and Flexing Fall.
As Summer lifts her skirts
to ascend heaven,
Fall descends
to wrestle her down,
the two locked
in warm-cold embrace
like Jacob and his god.
November-morning gray
hangs listless and heavy
over the lawn. The sparrows
in retreat number in the hundreds,
their small heads bobbing,
beaks like machine needles sharp,
threading their lunches
to feed their flight.
Southward bound, they were
before this stop, a measure
against the inevitable winds
rising broadside to their journey.
No real clue to immediate
outcome, but Summer will not
turn her back on Fall again
until December.

THE MAJESTIC OAK

Sad, a tree or a man struck down in his prime.
Workmen were there early morning
topping, cropping lower limbs all the way down.
The prisoner stood awaiting execution,
stripped of all respect,
its limbs scattered below in pieces,
pale stubs where strong limbs had grown.
October lightning had skinned
the south side, splintering a limb
and flinging it two houses down.
I have always wondered why lightning
chooses its foe in a tree.
Stately the full-grown oak
had stood in its prime, maturing
each spring with greater majesty,
drinking thirstily of the sun's wine.
Out my kitchen window, the sky hangs
too low, too bare, the sun too harsh.
No longer is there a green trellis
on which to spread my thoughts; thoughts out
the window now have nothing to climb.
They took away the pieces of the oak today.

BALLERINAS IN DISGUISE

How like ballerinas
these three myrtles were,
each stretching its limbs
toward azure sky,
creating the illusion
of three dancers, their
burnished pewter and ivory trunks
in sculptured beauty dressed.
That I had caught the three
in their dance routine thrilled me.
But I was not privy to their green sphere,
and they quickly returned to their showy
stance of soft pink and ivory gray.
What but for their own private dance
did they exercise so cheerfully
and secretively in the hot June breeze,
waving their limbs full of billowing
pink chiffon above me.

DEBT TO NATURE

Long lost, overturned in a thrust
of playful wind among tall oak offspring,
family sweet gum and pine, you lie
under the shaded morning sun, face down
like a clipped kite, a home now for more
organisms than there are people on earth.
Were you aware of your debt to nature,
loose, shallow-rooted oak, when you
collapsed, selectively fell in stunt, in play,
found yourself on ground at God's ear?
Toppled, now leafless, indecent—
nature doesn't mind when her workers
are grinding ground you once stood on.
Only your world-sized trunk of broken brown,
scattered, blotched limbs, gray, resting on
sun-dried wood chips remain after years
in moldy decay of fragile balance.
Hundreds, thousands, even more driven
by need, competition, greed
squirm, slide, crawl, run along
your sun-bleached, bark-blotched sides.
A voiceless black snake—within carcass
live inhabitants in dwellings engraved
like ancient cave dwellers, furrows occupied,
some empty, well-laid ant factories for tour,
grub notches as nurseries, billions mill solitary,
single file, mall wide in every direction,
segregated by phylum, order, family, genus,
species—and I, a peep. When I compare
my debt to yours, felled tree, I wonder
at my worth, my credit worthiness—the number
I consume—and I likewise consumed—
to keep the life cycle going.
Tell me again that death
is the wages of sin. Tell me
the sin of this oak.

DOVE

The thud heard 'round the world
heralded a stunned bird. A clever
hawk had confused a young dove,
driving her into the keeping-room window.
On the grass, the young dove lay motionless.
Attempts to check her injuries
caused her to flee into the flowerbed.
Up above, the hawk circled the sky looking
for his prey. Human presence caused him
to settle nearby on the neighbor's rooftop.
The night slowly cloaked the area for her safety.
The next morning, the big hands that grabbed her
and took her to safety must have seemed to be
the monster in the sky she so feared.

JAM

Yesterday, I looked in my refrigerator
to see a fungus nibbling my jam.
The gray, smutty blob that began
as a tiny gray pea spread like cold syrup
at first; then like hot chocolate,
it spread more until today …
when I looked in my refrigerator
again to see my jam gone
and a fuzzy fungus in its realm.

VISITOR

In an instance,
like a misguided dart,
he landed quickly-green
upon my windowsill.
Three rapid push-ups later,
he grew steadily-brown.
As I leaned nearer,
he quizzed, cocked his head
toward mine,
and turned
craftily
still.

JUBILANCE

In Louisiana November, the fountain gurgling
air-refreshed water is a strong temptation for visitors.
As temperatures climb to high eighties,
the water is the backdrop for a party. Fluffing out
their feathers, dancing their struts to send
the water cascading from the fountain mouth
closer to their bodies, they splash water over the sides,
then dart into the azaleas to preen their feathers.
Refreshed for the trip to warmer climates,
they have disappeared in unison on their journey south,
and their absence remains as the cooler air swirls.

SKINK

The cold front has brought much-needed rain.
And cooler temperatures make another sighting
unlikely of this arboreal creature. He has built
his playground in the hollow limbs and cavities
of the hardwood at the edge of the property.
The skink in his tight brown suit collaring
his red, swollen jaws and throat has stepped out
from the cluster of azaleas and hardwoods.
The shy creature pauses momentarily to sun himself
on a warm brick and to check the neighborhood
from the patio of his apartment. He pauses for one
last look and then withdraws, leaving only his head
showing through the open window in the bricks.
All that remains with the season's change:
his image now on the iPhone.

SPRING PARADE

Down the unkempt lane they come:
trees making merry, budding
in parade, all drunk from nature's rum,
rocking rhythmically in the soft breezes of spring
nudging outward, limb lengths to each other.
Magnolias attired in wide skirts of glossy green
dwarfed by live oaks marching boldly in myrtle,
crowded by orphan water oaks underfoot in green and yellow.
Cypress, in its lacy filigree skirts of emerald,
elm, green ash, pines in dark green for all to see
take best in show but move slowly to mirth,
followed closely by silver maples and river birch
flashing the silvery whites of their underskirts.
All swaying above the carpet of harlequin green,
filling the lane in shades of spring.

ODYSSEY

The autumn sun burns low in the west.
The red, yellow, magenta leaves
drop like amateur parachutists
from the fibrous ceiling of trees.
For weeks, falling leaves have gathered
along the banks of the drifting stream
like spectators watching a tennis match.
Many leaves fall midstream and sweep past,
much like downhill skiers, sure and confident,
curling edges to make the turns,
straightening effortlessly on exit—
champions in human terms. Just so,
others slip in on waking breezes,
drifting to waiting traps of fallen tree limbs
like an audience leaving the theater. Still others,
riding a harsher gust, slide recklessly into whirlpools
to be spun around without end like reckless racers.

THERE, THEN NOT

In the warm afternoon November sun,
hundreds of blackbirds descended,
dotting recently mowed green grass black.
Fifty in sleek, dark business suits
worked to clean blades of grass like store managers
straightening displays for customers. In the fountain,
six or so of the privileged splashed in the water
and took sips from around the rim of the pool.
As if choreographed, all rose in unison,
and the grass was green again
in the warm afternoon November sun.

THE LONELY SENTINEL

The golden patina of the evening sun
softly cloaks the tall pines
as the lonely sentinel stands
surrounded by its tasseled charges.
Its uniform of multicolors
drapes loosely about the plank figure
with one arm dropped and the other
in permanent salute. On its head
rests the stained gray fedora.
The enemy sits in rows along the barbed wire.
Without consultation, one daring crow
swoops, rising above the figure
as if riding a skateboard
up a bank of air,
then in slow motion
cascades down upon the crown
of the floppy-brimmed hat.
As if by some unseen signal,
joining the first is another
on the upturned arm, a beckon to all,
making a mockery of the farmer's efforts
and making fair game out of nature's
bountiful crop of corn.

EPIPHANY

The day hardly seems the same
as first begun—the redbud's leaves
are paling in the cool October
morning gray sun.
The graying oh so slight
that I do not notice before
the dying in me
until in this tree I see
green polychromes
in clean, moist air—
green paling, green yellowing
tenuous ornaments where
nervous rain crystals cling.
Clouds hail north
like large cotton puffs
conveyed in a time warp.
A matter of years makes
a great difference; a decade
can leave its mark;
even a moment,
then everything speeds up—
fast motion—or you realize
it's been fast motion,
and you slow before you know.
Here in the windowpane,
maturity looks back
from my father's eyes,
their expressions somehow
my mother's freed.
Her cheekbones and smile:
my consummate self
reflecting their union,
and their winter graying too.
On paling yellow leaves,

on these my hands, both age
naturally in this process
under the falling gray sky
in the coming night.

THE STUFF OF MIRACLES

Dead center: a descent from above.
Between me and the four o'clock sun's glow,
a vortex of red, orange, yellow,
a sunburst of miracle I thought was
but a tallow tree leafed in sunlight.
At once I knew I was the child still
crouched by the glowing embers
of a late-afternoon fire,
poking burning limbs and underbrush
cut in a day's clearing. Swelling with air
ready to burst orange-red, the embers
expelled the ancient mysteries
of the burning bush, sending off
starry sparks as the fire breathed
hot into the cool night air.
A piece over, by the deep-cut clay gulley,
red river clay was strong enough
to breathe life into, more smoke
from the last burning,
from under the pines
that had never feared flooding
and knew only fire walking.
I watched the stars poke through
night's cloak and wondered
at Jacob's courage, dreaming
to wrestle the Reader of Palms,
the Counter of Sparrows.
What I had hoped for was
never more than
the thrill of knowing …
I would never know
beyond the day
the measures of the mind
that carries the divining rod,

that reads the tea leaves
and believes in water witching.
The flames with the stars
under colorful leaves showed
as bright as melting gold.
I stood once again that late afternoon,
looking still at breathing
red, orange, yellow melting sun glow.

NATURE'S CHAPEL

When the trees grow restless
and sway their limbs
to the music of the wind,
or in the late afternoon
when the mockingbirds scale
the drifts of the rooftops
to chastise the cat,
or when every whisper of the breeze
promises mysteries pushing burdens away,
I know I am in nature's chapel
under the umbrella
of dogwood and Chinese elm.

THE VISIT THAT WAS

She stands at the sink in the kitchen
dressed in white jeans and a man's shirt,
her hair lightly peppered with gray.
She prepares for the rolling of biscuit
dough for chicken and dumplings.
She does not hear me enter, but sensing a presence
only she might know, she turns, her face aglow.
                    "When did you get in!"
My memories are solid, good ones.
The kitchen has changed little since my youth.
Varnished pecan cabinets form an *L*.
The sink faces southeast, an appropriate spot
for the woman who waited and watched
for each spring's early birth of daffodil and narcissus.

MYSTERY

Sister found such mystery
in life. At three, she asked,
"Who made me?" and at four
declared she'd eat no more
carrots for her eyesight:
"One for this eye; one for this."
Mom and I smiled knowingly
at her querulous stance
when, with hands on hips, she'd declare
some truth she'd found
playing in the cool sand,
as in the hot spring morning
during planting season
when she lingered farther and farther
behind, exploring the intricacies
of the newly plowed earth,
neatly parted in fresh rows.
Seeds were scarce, and one was
all that was needed,
our parents had explained.
Enough would come up from one,
and then there'd be none to thin.
But Sister pored lovingly
over each hole made by Mother's hoe.
Hurry! Hurry! we'd think,
but we said not a thing,
for we knew Sister gave
each seed a mate.
Two seeds to a hill—
one to grow, one to wait.

CONFESSIONS OF A FIRSTBORN
(FOR MARY JO JOHNSON PERRITT)

A Cherokee maiden, I imagined,
as she moved so quietly, so wisely,
as she methodically worked
the biscuit dough at daybreak.
She was the woman who earned
my years from seventeen of her own
as she beat her wash on the river rock
while the sun sipped the dew from the leaves.
As I grew from her feet to her side,
I watched her spin my youth
in her youthful eyes, in Easter lily white
and blue organza eyelet, chiffon bows and pearls.
How I marveled at her barbed assurance
when I asked and she'd say,
"Ol' wives' tales. That's all."
With her energy, she could
birth a calf, mend a fence,
bale hay on scorching August days.
Dressed loosely in men's clothing,
straw hat, work boots, without gloves.
Self-doubt she spurned for what had to be done.
On acres of cattle range, pine trees, and corn,
in the beauty of frost, cool morning dew
of daffodil and dew cup, of life's wisps,
she taught me all. The woman who dotted
my i's with praise for every unsure thought
is the woman who taught me life.

WISP OF TRUTH

The round white wisp
fascinated the toddler.
With one quick snatch,
she was running in the hot afternoon sun,
running against the hot breeze
and the sting of knee-high weeds
in a surge of self. The wispy dream
in her hand floated apart, leaving
only a particle or two attached to stem.
Perplexed, she turned to look
at another wispy structure,
but this time, she did not touch.
Early in this child's life,
reality settled into her free spirit
with a hush.

DECLARATION

I love you.
I love you true.
I love you. I do. I do.
I love the way
you say you love me too—
that I may stay my icy feet
against your warmth,
set the thermostat for morn
and evening for return home,
heat the water for a cup of tea.
I love you true.
I do. I do.

I love you.
I love you rude,
even when in traffic
you come unglued
and just as quickly
brush my cheek with
the back of your hand.
With self-restraint, you understand.
I love you. I do.
When I swear the worst
is many and you say,
"Ah, it's but few."

I love you.
I love you light,
when your humor
stays my day's blight
with carpet stained,
ice maker iceless,
budget too tight,
egg cracked in newly

bought dozen.
You smile,
and I love you again.
I do. I do.

THE GIFT

It came with a broken top
and missing stems, with limbs

reaching forward for the light as if blown
by some wayward wind, stretching

for the sun as a child, as a dancer
for the dance. The misshapen poinsettia

you rescued from an office party two years ago
and brought to me has remembered

its purpose and is dancing in red.
Each day, the plant has leafed red

from the green butterfly form,
the butterfly leaves on each stem

billowing out in a scarf dance.
The red leafing of green has evolved

into a natural dance with the light.
Still in the container and soil of its birth,

its daily chances have brought it closer to
what it was meant to be. Inching outward

each day, the butterfly clusters have become
four and six and eight more until now the process

is nearly complete. The poinsettia you rescued
and brought to me dances happily in full gala

at my arbor door window, a rescued soul
that now gives new spirit and heart with its dance in red.

(Previously published in *Black & Rouge Review* 2, no. 1, Spring 2009)

STATUS CHANGE

It was laughter; it was tears,
that state of happiness
a temporary state of ice.
So cold it burned.
So extreme it ruined
from too little talk—
or was it too much?
Its permanence
like an exploding Roman candle,
multitudinous in effect like
Fourth of July fireworks,
evanescing from the coalesced,
itself no longer. A house emptied,
cabinets bare, one glove left,
one shoe in the corner,
one of the pair no longer there.

MUDDY WORDS

I have collapsed into myself
like a downed parachute.
Today, I learned you choose
another with whom to wear
the words, the lies.
The red one would make
such an attractive tie.
The black or gray one,
such a nice suit, you know—
the bleached one,
a stiffly starched shirt.
Wear them well—
as well as ever,
I'm sure.
But what if this time
she notices muddy words
on your shined shoes
and knows you
for what you are?
And what if this time
you want to come back,
and what if this time
I take matters into my own hands?
Words have no class,
or they have it all—this time.

A MATTER BEST NOT DISCUSSED

A matter best not discussed
is a matter you sit alone with
on a slow night watching
the season's reruns. If you
dare to peer from
your darkened house
to the well-lit street,
matters that make your
stomach curdle, your heart
race, your curiosity swell
consume you or begin
like sleep in the foot working
up to eat your heart raw.
That's a little like what happens
during a hormone surge in the middle
of the night, setting you
searching for meaning
everywhere, anywhere—
in the refrigerator for leftovers,
in a cup of chamomile tea,
in the back issues stacked
a foot high on the coffee table.
Flipping the pages, I think
of sitting on my restless haunches
and baying at the frothing moon
arching lunar arrows invisible
to all nerves and heart,
vein and vine. The pink, sweet
swelling expelled from double-hung
pods now rides thin, starchy
waves of warm protein. At this
point, you wish for design
to quicken the pace of
cool blue-green release,

warm flesh spinning, flipping
morning egg bright and fresh
under moonlight. Choice divides
confidence, strips growth on vine.
Red plum, blue ripe round:
life-form by air unbound until
cocoon unfolds in blood warmth,
the child of lung and heart.
Body moon moves again
over mind mass, pulling waves
warm over my body chaste.

PARTNERS, NOT FRIENDS

Partners we have become
in the kitchen, as one.
You slice the lettuce;
I brown the meat.
You chop the tomato.
I add the seasonings
and methodically lower the heat.
You grate the cheddar;
I add more water to the meat.
As the steam rises lazily
from the steeping tea,
the timer expires,
and it's lunch.
Ice cubes thump the tea,
and the tea responds,
"This friendship has limits."

IT TAKES TWO

I pick up the book to read and put it down
to notice I have only moved the bookmark
to the next page. I am as jumpy as a thought
perched on the edge of a hot skillet.
If it takes only one, a bad apple, a good egg,
why can't I settle this argument within myself?
Why is what I have and know not enough?

By day, I strain my words of disappointment
in my tea. I pick up the phone to dial a friend's number.
I steep another tea bag instead and gaze out the window.
Outside, the blue jay clatters in curses I hear in my head.
Mischievous grass grows without regard in the flowerbeds.
To escape the heat, dried leaves curl upward in fragile spirals.

It takes only one, a bad apple, a good egg.
The thought that occupies me now—
that the one who possesses
both stands best against the wily winds
to understand or label someone else
with dismissive doubt.

At dusk, trees crowd 'round like spectators
for a night game in the late evening.
The sky peers back in starlit winks.
Momentary heat relief from moist lips
of faint breezes brushes against my skin
with coolness, yet no relief from searing shards
of doubt of what it would take to make this one right.

FADING FRIENDSHIPS

The moment from nowhere
brought a thought to mind
of friendships past, of clearer days
and spindles yet to untwine
the kind often left to test,
when friends touch our lives
and warm our thoughts,
when you rolled my sleeves
with assurances that the sweater looked better
and eased the tension with the quiet "Now."
We do miss each other, we tell ourselves,
when busy friends fade away.

THE MUTE FRUIT

The red fruit's mute.
I sit in the dark.
You switch on the light.
You think you are helping.
I want to sit in quiet
without man-made sight.

I think and read.
You intercede to ask
where is where
and what is what or
this or that—
will I look?

I write.
You interrupt—
You tease my thoughts
and do fast footwork,
midair antics to steal
my insight.

What! Here again!

AN OPEN LETTER TO ADRIENNE RICH

Someone else has already spoken.
Someone else has already nailed
the truth to the yoke, posted it
like a No Trespassing sign, a crux.

Had I known this truth, newly found,
from which to build my own,
I would not want to return
to Eve's first garden of apple trees
to eat the apple again with one big,
deliberate bite, then in twenty nibbles,
peeling skin and pulp down to the core
to check Lucifer's Promethean disguise.

This time, I would not tell Adam. I
would cavort with this god, this
serpent man, behind Adam's back,
relive the two millennia to see
if it makes a difference,
a better or lesser god, this time in Adam.

(Previously published in *Black & Rouge Review* 1, no. 1, Spring 2008)

HEARTBREAK

Removed,
he
became,
and
I
remained.
Love
disappeared
in the crack
of a lightning bolt
the day
the threat
to
my heart
was
named.

THE NECKLACE

For this costly gift,
the proper exchange was a piece of heart,
sliced off on the cutting board of commitment.
A golden iris pendant, a pearl center,
a diamond for accent in a twist of gold,
curled, sleeping like a serpent
in my jewelry drawer,
a twisted human relic of memory
woven into a bird's nest.
A circle of memories covering
the floor of my mind the way a fog
hugs the lowland. I drape the chain
across my fingers only to watch it
curl around and slip to the carpet.
Disheveled drawers full of damp memories
spill their contents, falling to the floor breathlessly,
crying out for rescue. December wind was blowing
from the north as the car rattled down the empty street.
Christmas lights warmed the night.

SILENCE

Are you waiting for me to speak—

hot to cold to equilibrium
emotional entropy to maximum order

                    too few moments to recall

Are you waiting for me to say—

mysterious and colorful stars
dance in distant magnetic explosions

                    too few sightings to detect

Are you waiting for me to tell—

Arctic ice caps melt as desert shrubs
in climate rage creep up the slopes

                    too few words to resist

Are you waiting for me to declare—

Hanssen's national betrayal's complete and
the sphinx sings alone in the arms of the desert

                    too few dirges to remit

These questions have crystallized in my mind
like calcium deposits in soft tissue, a sediment,
and I frolic madly on this crowded stage.
The rage remains, unanswered and untested.

(Previously published in *Black & Rouge Review* 2, no. 1, Spring 2009)

CLARITY

Storm clouds are clearing early evening.
In the distance, thunderclouds grumble in soft rumbles.
The rain has formed small puddles in low spots.
The air smells as fresh as rosewater in tea.
Tired now from prancing, limbs of the elm slow.
In this summer wind and rain, nature has bathed all.
On the branches, the birds are singing once again,
sizing up the results of the sport.
All is regrouped, organized, dried, and dusted.
The storm has cleared my mind and given me
the courage to bevel the edges of my thoughts and
miter the corners of my memory, separating and
framing the old from the new.
Nothing comes easy.
Nothing comes quickly.
I have given up on you.
I am giving you up.

THE ANSWER

I have only one life to live, and I
take Malamud's advice:
"We have two lives, the life we learn with
and the life we live with after that."
If I had two hearts,
I'd dedicate the paper heart
to a double life on a two-way street
until the choice is too uncertain.
Paper hearts love paper roses
and paper dolls on a slippery stage
where luck can go wrong. A waterfall
of drowning doubt breeds fear
of washing away the rules of the game.
Instead, to place this paper heart on the shelf
is to keep a candle in the dark and
a paper tiger safe to cry
at the paper moon.

SIGHTING

In the vortex of late-afternoon rain,
pelted with emotion and delusion,
I caught a semblance of you.
There, in front of me,
he, the receding hairline and
the angular stride. His friendly
gaze saw, too, something in me.
The swirling mental fog thickened.
I, immersed in a river of memories,
thrashing to turn back into
the protective cocoon of reality.
I watched as he rounded the corner
of the building and disappeared.
I thought you were in my heart,
volcanic and sporadic, now gone.

(Previously published in *Black & Rouge Review* 1, no. 1, Spring 2008)

THE STRANGER

I sometimes watch the stranger in him
as he searches his memory
for the answer to some problem
he has brought home from work.
I see a stranger, too, in him,
who stops when shopping to touch
a figurine or
who furrows the brow
as he replaces the credit card
in his wallet.
I see him withdraw to pure pleasure
as he rolls an ice-cream cone
around on his tongue.
He glances up and around;
I catch his eye, and
he comes back to me.

POSSIBILITIES

If only I were you
and you were me,
would we, could we,
see the best,
the worst,
and forgive each
for what it's worth?
Forget the close ones;
let go the worst,
grow, and more.
If one I were,
if two were you,
everybody else could be three.
Three or more,
but we would not care anymore.
All for one
and one for all,
in the rise or in the fall,
straight to the edge
and back again.
What fun!
        If only I were you
and you were me
and everything else were rosy.

THE SCHEME OF THINGS WITH GRANDJEAN

Sun-dried memories hang
like khaki work shirts
in warm jasmine breezes.
The young dreams keep
like dry goods sold
among the tales told
of the endless walks and
incessant talk. With cane
in hand to steady thoughts,
he ferrets out the sun flashes
on broken glass or discarded
bridle rings, to follow through
the grasses the glide of the garter snake,
or to trail a hawk in flight.
I, there to ask the four-year-old's questions:
Why the moon? And the man's face therein?
Where will you go when you die?
Slowed steps and unsteady hands,
the need to rest under the apple blossoms
until the spring to the step returns
to take us back to the front-porch evenings:
he, in his rocking chair; I, in mine;
and the final answer in the moon
and the face there etched
in the memories spun like spiderwebs hung.

THE UNEXPECTED
(IN MEMORIAM)

Twenty miles beyond city limits
to the country churchyard deep inside the woods,
thickets of curious spectators crowded
the roadway, expectant, and followed
the hearse from hill to hill. Thirty years
of overgrowth had left them
thick and deep, tall sentinels at watch
over the gray casket covered in red carnations.
The heavy, humid July air hung
in clumps of life-choking moss. And I,
with nowhere to turn, held back
the swelling tears as the minister's
words slipped past me into vacuity.
The meaning of his death
eluded me, leaving only grief
to quell my heart until, as if on cue,
the towering pines eased aside,
allowing a soft, solitary breeze
to welcome him home.

POSTCARD
(FOR VICKIE)

Your African violet is still lovely.
I hope I did not annoy you
with my suggestions for care.
Actually, instead of too much light,
the plant may need more light.
I have it now in a west window.
It may be looking better.
I like your plant. I will keep it
for you until you are again settled.

POETESS

Down
the life shoot
billions of years
long
mortal body
pregnant
with immortal kind
dropped
to find
all was not ready.
An alien
of kind
in a climate
too stale,
a world
too raucous
for the senses
turned
the visitor
winded
and pale.
The small body
shriveled
as customary
to human fine
and left after
five decades
and six years
to return up
the misty
mountainous climb
where
surely
she's found

home
by now.
Dare I
think so?
Will we,
Emily,
ever know?

PROTÉGÉ
(FOR JOSEPHINE FOSTER)

Her voice flowing from the past
mellows on the surface of the sounds
from Spanish guitar, Indian flute,
jaw harp, and Raramuri Indian violin:
the sounds of woodland streams happy with birds,
the peace of stillness in the pines,
the wobble of gypsy jazz, a flamenco flavor.
The sound of an angel's voice sent from
the kingdom of heaven and inspired
by a Verdi aria labeled arresting,
she says vibrating, depending
on strum, ping, and whine of the jaw harp
and the Spanish guitar. From an earlier, bluesy time,
floating from the cool of porch recordings,
coming from another, borrowed from La Argentita,
her vibrating voice promises to be borrowed
through time by a new voice, your voice.

OUT OF THE BLUE

Out of the blue
without warning,
a moment caught
in the throes
of a trance
in the cool
of a spring morning,
stopped in traffic
by the realization,
the need to protect.
A feeling screaming
against the moment,
rushing, flushing
the seconds through me,
through traffic, and I knew
you would not
be coming home
that evening.

UNNATURAL DEATH
(IN MEMORIAM)

The four o'clock sun was steady,
lengthening the shadows of the pines
along the thicket floor. From above,
a gliding hawk crisscrossed the pine straw.
Below, I watched as the corn snake moved
to the tree at the edge of the pines,
its periscopic head peering, rippling
body climbing the foot of the Florida pine
until all four feet wrapped, squeezed itself
off the ground and up the trunk. The snake
swung to the right, to the sunny side nearer
the woodpecker's nest. Head lobbing, straining
to free six inches more to explore the dark
hole in the side of the tree, the snake crashed
to the ground like a leafless limb. Only tree resin,
warm and sticky, purposely blessed, had slowed
the serpent's quest. The sound from the television
screen of its fall stunned me. I had watched death
creep upward from the coiled knot at the bottom
of your sad heart, slithering up and along the seams,
along the inside of your porcelain mask,
through hollow eyes, hollow mouth, smothering,
squeezing your pain, your cries, your last breath,
Little Bird.

(Previously published in *Black & Rouge Review* 1, no. 1, Spring 2008)

LUCILLE

She wears her ninety years with joy,
still pretty, petite, and positive in her svelte body.
She rolls her words in a humorous dough
that whets the appetite for more
and clings to the memory like German
chocolate icing—thick, smooth, and sweet.

A bad knee sticks to her walk in a swell each day.
Little else slows her. Practical in sets, she sent
her lover back to his family because of failing health.
Too much paperwork has prevented a legal union.
But his two trips to visit her in the hospital seem right.
She has survived two marriages and two stints. But
this time the medical news is grave: arteries clogged
in beaver-dammed streams; valve leaks
in a punctured tin can, coffee, a lost, inalienable right.

Too much medical paperwork has
stalled all for a nonagenarian moment.
She returns home to living once more,
where she finds life simple and fair
with Faith, her physician.

IN MEMORIAM

A. M.
RHS Senior
Died: February 9, 1986

No,
not often,
not once
in the last week.
From me,
you asked not
for a moment of my time,
five minutes,
a kind word,
a sympathetic ear,
my full attention,
a little understanding.
You left
without
an apology,
a good-bye,
without
closing the door
or the account,
without a forwarding address.
You demanded
a period to your sentence,
a full stop,
an end, my Silly Bird.
I thank you
for your refrain
that remains: "When the going gets weird,
            the weird get going."

MAJOR

One dew-cool Saturday morning,
before our parents were up,
we found Major down by the ditch
at the rear of the Cracker Barrel store.
Scraggly, yellow fur matted,
his pure, soft meow fell like cake crumbs
from his mouth, brought our tadpole hunt
to an end, and how! Home he went with us,
each jousting the other for a chance to carry him
for the next block. I swear he seemed to enjoy
the dissension he caused between my sister and me.
Hands lifted in protest, Mom took one look and said,
"I am going to hate him!" But we swept him up
and away, and through soft and pure reasons,
he stayed. Over the next few days, he rubbed
against Mom's leg and kissed her hand when
she fed, when we forgot or were too busy.
Soon he slept on Mom's bed.

SYNERGISM

In rhythmic swing,
perfect grace floats.
Down the sidewalk she comes
each afternoon on her furry pads,
so soft not a grass blade she breaks.
Forelegs swinging inward
like a California girl,
one foot, then the other
nearly in the same track.
Her hips swing in perfect synchronization,
a mermaid upright on fin.
Perfect motion, perfect form,
perfect grace, she lifts
her small, heart-shaped face
to yours, and all that is there are
the green cat eyes and her sonorous sound.

PREY

Head lifted toward her prey,
black fur dusted in camouflage sand,
blending clever with the concrete,
she paused. His half-hunched body agile
with disjointing accuracy,
he waited for the moment
when she would spring
with his idea to make
opportunity his own.
The intruder crept low on his belly
to the bench beside the table
where she waited. Intent,
she turned to deliver
one sharp squall, then back
to the stalking stance
to rise in controlled haunch
to reach the bird
on the arbor swing.
Dove in flight, her plan thwarted,
she growled at the tom,
the uninvited of her hunt,
of her heart, the foul to her and to her game.
Is it not so? Was it not so?
For Pankhurst, Jackson, Gunning, and Wiggins
in hunts for survival, sustenance, self?
Did not the toms thwart
or seize the glory of the hunt?
And cut out woman's heart?

SU-MING

Does she live vicariously,
or is she a poet?
She whose beauty
like that of black onyx
in regal porcelain poise lies,
body folding over porch rail
like soft licorice. She,
whose curious eyes,
like greenish-yellow cabochon-cut
chrysoberyls, watch early-morning joggers
and robed early risers securing
garbage cans at the curb.
Watchful eyes never pausing
until morning slows and
she places her head, chin first,
on her left forepaw
to remember the poems
of a feline goddess,
to dream Bastet's dreams.

DÉTENTE

Through wordless moves, she spoke
as she flipped her hind self east,
her front self west,
back and forth,
wrenching, wringing
twice more her body,
the passion for conquest.
"Come join me," she wooed.
"Come a little closer,
won't you?" echoed her moves.
"Kist! Kist! Kist!"
the mockingbird threatened
through clenched beak
as he hopped twice west
and then east stepped,
gesturing in terms to protect his nest.
The cat flipped south to face the bird
and watched instead its flight.
Without regret, she rolled over to rest—
the end of a summit, no doubt,
between east and west.

DREAMERS MAKE GOOD POETS
(FOR HIGHIE H. PERRITT)

From the roadside, as far as he could see,
encroaching green thickets collared
the sunbaked and weed-strewn farmland
the way the years had crowded him.
His family of six, three girls and two boys,
a wife, always seemed to crowd him.
In fact, for a sensitive man like himself,
living with himself was like being
in a vise, pressed constantly from all sides,
like the isolated clusters of bitter weeds
to be cut before they ruin the cow's milk.
Surprising, he found it:
that a lifetime passes as quickly
as the grazing seasons on the grasses,
turning the cows in to graze,
turning the cows out to pasture—
there in the neighboring field
were the two cows now kept
for milk and beef calves.
What was it, anyway, that would force
a dreamer like himself
into such a hard existence?
Even his body protested the soil and the pollen.
He felt a cool breeze
that rose from nowhere,
shaking the sycamore's leaves like chimes,
reminding him that he had much to speak of—
more acreage than most these days
and five kids who seemed to make their way,
mostly without his aid,
and a dedicated woman, still mysterious
in her own right. The kids, in fact,
found him hard to understand—he was

like everybody else—he wanted
a good living for his family,
at least one new car in his lifetime.
Why was this so hard for them to understand
about an honest, hardworking man like himself?
Oh, if anyone would ask—
and he wished someone would—
he had made the big mistake
over forty years ago.
Dreamers don't make good farmers.
Farming calls for practical men
who are always tough under the hot sun.
He had tried to be tough.
Dreamers, he knew, make good poets,
philosophers, and sometimes, good teachers.
Well, anyway, seated in his straight back
under the sycamores, he had realized
everything—maybe he had them all—
the dreams … every dream any man could imagine—
just maybe … and who was wealthier
than a man who can allow himself
to dream, sitting on soil
he has owned outright for years?

THE POET

I saw a poet unfolding,
first from the truth unmolding,
germinating from the knowing
of the treachery of growing.
From within to begin
the magic, the first line
silently glowed
like incandescent chalk
on an otherwise-clean poetic slate.
From the brain node
to the nerves
rode the emotions
in self-doubt
yet clearly a notion
to let out
finally
in an emotional
manifestation.

(Previously published in *Black & Rouge Review* 1, no. 1, Spring 2008)

QUEST
(FOR KRISSI)

An aversion she had felt
when she herself first met.
Beginning unsure when from
pod-sleep woke, titters from
the red-pulsed chute slipped
to homestead under heart.
The tattered truth imprisoned her
in white light. She felt for months
the lump-sized, stone-cold peal,
stinging deep within like
a nectar-dining bee, in
sleeping gales floating from
yawning grooves. Waking masks
mocked, curling to flatten in her chest.
Blue-bruised piercing over
ancient ashes fed dancing
blue-yellow-red fire blades
along fear's edge. Those who knew
could have told. There was little
to do but wait. The mariposa mirth, now
the mirrored thirteen years
before her stood, every woman's laughter
no longer a stranger. Long gazes
into the mirrored summer eyes
wed familiarity now, not contempt.
From the passion-filled mouth,
each day with each look,
jubilance slipped. She found herself
between twelve and sixty-five, smiling,
knowing laughter full-grown
had found home.

IMAGE OF STYLE
(FOR BARBARA)

Dots of color on the wings of words
coalesced to form her image
on the TV monitor—amazing,
she thought, how easily
she assumed the spot.
Talking on camera,
they told her, is an art,
yet the red cuing light
during taping set the words
gliding off her tongue,
out of their launch, gliding
glibly from point to point
as if from an Aspen peak.
She felt the cool flush
as she heard her words carry
the snowy truth about
suicide and dying.
She knew her stuff.
She always did. Later
that same day, family
and friends, sounding
somehow surprised, would say,
"You were so good!"
"I didn't know you were *that* good!"
Ah, the accord of a family
and friends to see her
as they think she is. For
a day or two to them now,
she exudes a special peace—
echoes of a new self—
as she continues to make toast,
to remind, to teach, to counsel
in the lack of time. But she is
as she is as she was as she can be—
a myriad image of unforgettable style.

MAKING A LIVING SOMEHOW

"Just trying to make a buck,"
she would say
on those hot June–July days
during summer canning season
when the heat would force
no dog or cat
from under the shade.
Her saying usually went
"an honest living," but
she did not always make
the distinction. Honest,
hard work was what had
sustained her. During
canning months when the heat
wavered between ninety and one
hundred three, the Bible salesmen
would walk along the sides
of the parish road from town,
stepping through the steam
rising from the asphalt
as if disciples along
the River Jordan. There they
stopped—always—in front
of her screened door
just this side of the city-limit sign,
standing there in their city suits,
their product in hand, while the
sweat trickled down their young faces
like icing on a hot cake,
staining the tight collars
on their starched white shirts and
spreading in a wet yoke around
their shoulders. "Ma'am," they'd say,
straight from Bible college,

"does your family have this book of the Lord?"
implying, it seemed, that the family Bible
was not good enough and that the Lord
would approve of only the new and the best.
Not waiting for her answer, they'd continue
about the fine red, white, and black leather
binding choices, the gold-tipped pages
and indexed books in the new St. James version.
Sending them away with "I'm not interested
in your Bibles," she would turn from the door,
wiping sweat from her upper lip,
and say, "Guess we all have to make
a living somehow," and return
to shelling peas and skinning
blanched tomatoes, tasks she would
have completed before the
suffocating heat inebriated her,
had not the well pump lost its prime
and the neighbor's bull not torn
down the old barbed wire
to the heifers and the liniment salesman
and the burial policy collector not interrupted
her work trying to make a buck,
as Mary Jo put it, leaving out the honest part.

MONTH OF A LIFETIME

You would find him alone
sitting under a large sweetgum
on a piece of unsplit firewood
whittling with his pocketknife.
As skittish as an untamed cat, he would sit,
examining the piece of wood in deep thought before
his knife began peeling away the layers. You could
not say that he carved out anything recognizable.
He had returned from the Second World War unable
to remember a month of his experiences. He did not
know how to explain it. Neither did the VA. He had
lost a part of himself, gone forever in the jungles
of the South Pacific. She did not recognize the one
who had left her two years earlier by draft
and returned only with the nightmares of terror.

A YOUTH I MET

His thoughts play tag
like giddy schoolchildren at recess,
leapfrogging over one—then the other—
while he obsesses and selects the best.
The half-completed statement
"I—well, no, I won't say that"
reveals the constant battle
to delete the rest—
the honest thoughts and emotions
and any other silly notions.
Most utterances he labels *not good enough*,
especially his own, as he searches deep
to modify the content and the tone.
He faces life's daily choices,
mining for his truth, which he
has not realized rests uncovered
in perfect form, entwined in his youth.

WINDING MANNER

Raven haired is she
who flared brazen at times
to let the rest know
what she knew to be in store.
Strike her hot, no bind would find,
for she's more like a high-strung filly
in throws. She holds her truth inside
and feeds it her story for comfort.
The melody of the work calms her,
but she never gives in to the silence.
She is in control of herself, and
her barbs lie coiled, ready to strike.

BEQUEATH

Wait! Wait! I think. *Who should receive when things*
of the dead are divided? I watched as she moved
his wallet, leather belt, and tools to one side
for a brother and so on with other personal items.
The familiar smells of worn leather and shaving cream
permeated the folds of my memory,
while to another brother, his pocketknife,
his watch. I looked on as she moved his pocket possessions
to the side in a biblical divide, an abyss wider
than it seemed, and my thoughts tumbled into the empty hole,
whirling and spinning out of control.
My silent thoughts were never to find freedom
from the want for something to hold, to remember
him by. I study the face of his sister
in the photograph I brought home.
Some say I resemble her.

THE WEIGHT OF WORDS

A light rain is falling
around Catfish Town.
The voice on the radio fades
into my own as I try
to feel the rain,
to breathe the freshness.
But here in this house,
the air is tight,
suffocating, stretched
thin like the skin
of a balloon. Impostors,
these words: smoking memories
that hang and lie in grayness
all around me.

"A man is as good as his word,"
my father once told me, so
this relationship is over,
yours and mine; I know it.
I can give myself all the reasons.
The sounds of breathless words
are everywhere, in every room,
every memory—
in the children's clothes
to be folded,
the bathwater,
in the lather
of the soap bar.

Words once soft
as a drizzle
and moist, floating
on dragonfly wings,
brave and exciting,

curling 'round my marriage finger
in bands of silver and gold, then,
in a flash flood, so frightening.
Yours. Mine. Ours.
Washed away in a downpour,
in a flood of darkness
and salty tears;
flipping backward
on the slip of the tongue,
somersaulting to splat
like a rock in mud.

Deep, deep to the core,
planted words like seeds,
timed land mines,
geysers erupting
at midnight, breakfast, Sunday dinner—
that personal hell into which
you descended and the double-edged
words from the fire
that rose to slash my warm heart.

RESIDUE

Charging words in stampede
have left pockmarks filled with salt
on the face of the moon.
On my face, salty lies,
bitter to the tongue
as quinine.

Pebbles. Hail-stinging cold
on skin like a snapped rubber band.
When did the words become
simply technique, skill,
a product of lies—
"gifts," you called them—
your kill that I hung
with trust,
stuffed, mounted
ten-pointers
on the walls of this house,
now in my bed
where I lie.

YOUNG GRIEF

My grief is young still and demanding.
I must keep it close to my heart
like a good hand, lest someone notice
or peer to say that I must get out more,
fill my time with other things,
visit friends, or get on with living.
It's easier to say, "To live is to grieve."
There are days when I walk it to the window
to look for the promises of spring.
I must take it on spring walks in March
by the azaleas and quince showing.
Will I walk it too on the lazy days of June
to inspect the red salvia in hot sunlight
and the cool caladiums in the shade?
In the early evenings, I put down my reading
to show it the red sky in the west.
When night thickens, I explore the brilliance
of light and watch headlights from the passing cars.
I walk my grief to soothe it, talk to it
to understand, clutching it to me, rocking it,
humming to hush it.

My grief depends on me, and I must tend it to keep it cold,
else it will leave me hollow—I know.
It tugs at my day dress from the shadows
with the familiar face in the usual place,
with the voice, the walk—
My grief is young still,
and I must tend it.
I must place my rolled memories
on grief's fire until its coals
burn low below the cold,
leaving me warm again.

DOMINOES

Numbered, my days stand in rows
as far as the shadows recede,
as far as the light reaches.
Part illusion and part reality,
they stand only temporarily
before swept forward,
tipping over, one on the other,
setting all in motion,
rippling as far as time takes them
until all moments settle like dense fog,
indistinguishable and unnamed.
When day reaches tomorrow,
night will say I failed
to march my days in single file,
that I weaved in and out,
veering too far left and right.
Before this day's close, my days will stand
on end in ceremony for inspection,
and I will faint between the ends,
my reach too short, like that of a stunted vine,
my fall like that of a loosed rock in a mountain slide.
Trampling through the purple tunnels
of my sleep, they will pass,
marching, marching, marching.
Such urgency to hurry
to catch up, to keep step
with life, with pen—
as though there's too little time,
too few ideas. If I do not hurry,
someone else will win the race
to where I've already been.
Yet my pen waits
while my days tip in salute,
each to the other, falling like dominoes
in a sinuous ripple through time.

MUSE

I sought my muse in all the best places:
cool, quiet, sunlit beaches; fluorescent, bright spaces;
parks neatly trimmed; welcoming benches;
moments of warm rain; candy-pink blooms
of snarled myrtles in midspring,
blue lightning in a summer night's sky
above the tall, dark pines.
I did not know, did not understand,
until, without effort, it came to me
in a breath, and I sought to keep it
for myself. It grew beside me
like a beautiful mariposa lily
as from a cocoon, as colorful,
as fragile as butterfly wings, and
I yearned to possess it,
to walk it, show it, but it beat
against the glass prism of my heart,
too confined, too watched, too stroked.
I placed it on display along with the greeting
cards and dried rosebuds. Its beauty faded
until little truth was left, only gray powder.

POLITICS OF APOLOGIA

The silence is deafening in the deepening dusk.
I have always wondered who took the words
that left me mute, aborted my imagination
with the politeness of a smile
in the politics of apologia.
I thought you sincere.
How was I to know that only the trees
knew where the ransom lay, knew with whom, and
witnessed each day the new tricks strapped to mechanical breezes
swept along by the warm southern wind?
A greedy addiction that shames life itself—
I know my enemy. Yet the obvious is hard to see
deep within. I feel the rumbling of thunder from words
within that would shock you as you have shocked me
with your Janus eyes and Janus mouths.

FERVOR

Strange, the fervor with which
the new restores the old,
the fervor that grows
to salvage, to restore, to renovate
the dreams of Vitruvius.
It bugles forth a renaissance
of all that is classical past,
building with classic lines
and proportion, deemed historic
sites, created by ancient eyes and
critiqued by time. The soft
cudgeling of hammers,
the siren songs of workmen's saws
belay reality. Quarrelsome voices
drown the fuel of the tribal fires
threatening all that's salvaged and restored
until the voices of the chieftains ignite
the fires to burn a culture bright.
And the death winds blow,
sweeping up only to scatter more
falsehoods like dry leaves and loose grit,
fueling the darkest embers in us all.

CATHOLIC SCHOOL WEEK

A dilated lens clicks
to boundless rising
above the jubilance,
announcing
    the launching
of red, blue, green,
yellow, and purple
balloons
like pool balls
after the break shot
on the sky-blue tapestry.

SUMMER BREAK

Fluorescents quiet,
waste can spilling blight,
discarded binders and crumpled scribbles,
flags furled, waiting,
file drawers gaping,
overhead projector draped in black plastic,
gray cart posting "Send to the library."
Screen rolled, curled images from filmstrips,
two chalkboards—green, smeared, and streaked—
pencil sharpener dangling,
bookcases bare,
podium proudly scarred with carved initial C.
Students' desks, thirty lonely and pressed together for comfort,
teacher's chair seat splitting,
student desks cleaned of evidence, fingerprints, and the obscene
schoolroom closed for summer.

LEAVE ME TODAY

Leave me
today.
Watch
my shy eyes
turn away.
Do not
touch me,
not even
with your words.
Even kind ones
pucker
my tender skin
like green persimmons
on the tongue.
The swelling
in my head
flashes and threatens
like thunderclouds
on summer nights.
My sunburned
emotions,
so sore.
Let me be,
friend. Come by
another day.

IF I WERE

I stepped clumsily, fending off
cuts from pebbles sunning
under the rays that danced
along the water's edge,
fending off flashes
of pain and dying. Aggregation
of mental sediment, I am.

If I were a beaver

I would use my teeth
to chisel my housing from off the banks,
felling trees to build my fortress,
damming up the flow of these waters
near the mouth, fostering green growth
for a new spring, a new cycle,
a new course of affairs, a new life.

If I were an elephant

standing flat-footed,
I would not be threatened.
I would inundate myself with self-pleasure,
scooping snorts of warm, cooling waters
over my dry, hot body, my head
thrown back, trumpeting my pleasure
to the morning sun.

Or, were I the fiendish water snake

I would smile and stretch
out my five-foot-four length on the bank
until my blood warmed. I would slither
down the creek bank

like a woman and swim
to loosen my girth
before the hunt.

I went out early morning
wading the cool branch waters,
an imaginary pilgrimage in search
of myself, whether or not I learn to walk
the pebbles in this stream without pain, without pride.

GARDENER

The Gardener of Life prunes all
with lightning bolts of drought and disease,
thins and strips all from the grove as if weeds.
Some, like the crepe myrtles, grow statuesquely.
Some find it too much and are permanently stunted.
Some sprout incomplete from the nubs
of once limbs, and others sprout from the roots
over and over again as heroes.

COOL'S FACE

Oscillating face
turns
toward me.
Its cool breath
falls
short
as it
turns away
too quickly,
too shy,
yet curious
enough to return.

WINDOW SHOPPING

Once more, and I am out
window shopping—art nouveau, art deco—
clinging to sentiment, a triad of
yesterday, today, the moment.
Keeper of the pendulum whim,
who swings in shaded summer hammocks,
who rides the pendulum of the striking clock,
the rocking chair, unwinds the whims of warm hearts.
Memory lanes and jukebox,
bring back the young days,
young dreams, young hearts quivering
under the cool touch of flounced bedsheets
as a summer sprinkle stalls memory
where green hills and furrowed fields stand.
Seven miles of state highway and parish roads,
past watermelons and corn patches,
back to Road 34 between nowhere town and young fun,
                                    riding,
four girls in the black Chevrolet,
                        drinking
cherry Cokes and root beer,
                        floating
in the summer heat on ice-cream courage
to the beat of "See see rider, see what you've done now."
Giggles spin in wind-lashed hair across faces,
                            stringing
secrets, chatter, rock 'n' roll clatter
along the roadside on the way back to Nowhere Town.
Boyless, we'd squeal, whisper, laugh at a glance, and
hug the wheel.

At seventeen, sitting two, not four,
two-close, but three-less,
we four rode

separately
in boy-girl style.
Joyful, we imagined.
Friendless, I dare remember.

NIGHTMARE

Sh-h-h-h! I thought
I heard … I thought I heard a voice
dropping from distant clouds like lightning
in pink and orange neon flashes
carried on the fierce, hot wind
sweeping over the grayness
early in the rising up from
distant caverns in gray-blue fog.
There … there, I thought,
again circling the dark, low-lying trenches
where wiser thoughts have hidden …
But … it's gone—
swept away in freer winds,
dropped in flight
as quickly as grasped
like an eagle's poorly clasped
snare … Never mind …
Let me forget. It was a thought
calling my dare.

LOST WEEK

I found a stray week young in her days
and marked the find on the calendar.
Silver glitter, I, a skydiver
in kind wind, soaring and dropping
in an elaborate kite in free flight.
A butterfly, one diversion. A quick return,
a volley, and to the days
that followed with pressing matters.
In sleep, only dreams emerged
of cool nights, clear skies, and mimosa nights.
Slipping thoughts from my love's shirt pocket—until
the morning I saw unabashed, unabated week
and her strong days leap over
the graying cedar fence
and plunge into the neighbor's pool,
then out, dripping wet, to dry,
modified, and clinging to the fenders
of the car off to the next family's vacation.

A LOST THOUGHT

A thought I lost
I found today.
What is it they say?
About lost thoughts?
How do they get away
to be found back in place,
none the worse,
on another day?
Do they hail a ride
for a fast getaway or
jet away to another city?
Another sky?
Skydive to the bottom
of the cavern, or
fan out to escape recapture,
stealing away to foxholes
in the desert, or
scale the gray mountains
to safer heights?
Do they disguise themselves
as drunks, prostitutes, and bag ladies?
Do they hide behind the cloth?
Are they snatched half-green
by jealous gods' hands?
Come closer. I will tell you.
They play hide-and-seek
on the backs of fireflies
that flutter in the night.

MY POEM

The words have dried up,
brittle as pine straw, scorched by summer sun,
fragile as fleeting ashes of burning leaves.
They bud, but this drought leaves them
hanging on vines like dried string beans.
They rattle in the wind, empty and noisy,
dry and hard from lack of inspiration,
dried seeds in summer gourds of poetry.

WAKING LIVE

The will   to rage   against

                  death

   dissolves

                     in metaphorical tears, the cries of
       unwritten poetry

    amid vaporous thoughts,
        commoditized relations,

the constant presence of one instance, one-liners.

      Eternity resembles a wormhole

    in the waking hour of vacuous minds,

   the ongoing reality of the Elysian moment.

           You, the ancient mariner,

again

      on the high seas
         of wave-lashing verbiage,

  a long sleep-waking
     crying out for salvation,

         a second alarm call
    of the albatross.
Walking to mindfulness, I ask,
   "Is it subliminally or luminally dreaming?"

    Am I sleepwalking?

Is everything seen with human eyes rotoscoped   to make it believable?

Is it the ungluing   when Earth misses

    her groove
    in the turn
    of the spheres?
          From an ancient virus
    we may have come

all to learn as we sleep through the day or sleep through the night of our waking.

VACATION

In this zone, a glass of iced tea
slips unnoticed from the hand.
A long-awaited vacation frolics on the calendar:
white, sandy beaches along the Gulf of Mexico,
scattered umbrellas like red flowers in the sand.

The past three days have stretched
too long, like overused rubber bands,
as time stretches around lampposts
like youth eager for the night
in clothes in cycle spun tight.

Eager morning sun rises early through a crack
in the window blind and without a glitch retires
late to slip behind the tall pines. Afternoons
bathe in rays of sun or melt in rain, a biblical match
that holds the rising heat sane.

Inside, the house needs cleaning,
windows washing, lazy Susan moping;
the secrets of Cyclops's cave lie in the corner.
Thoughts derailed in a train of wet clothes
caught in spin, only a six-hour drive remains.

ALONE IN TRAFFIC

Cars in the early-morning haze
move along the four lanes
like dazed skaters gliding on ice.
Their occupants stare at the bumpers
of the cars ahead. The obedient slow
at the sight of the hanging red sphere
of energy, stopping. The occupant
in the inside lane stares straight,
perhaps at the sticker he sees that reads,
"Pray for the unborn." I cut my eyes
to the left in a daydream when the driver
looks my way. I direct my eyes away
along the sleek lines of his car,
from the back fender, back to front,
and then inside my car up to the
rearview mirror. I tuck a stray thought.
The traffic in the left lane strains and glides
once again. My momentary comrade
has moved slightly ahead, leaving me lonely.
Another takes his place. Escaping
the next traffic light but now rolling
at a snail's pace, I study the triangle
of brake lights on the car ahead,
reading, "Everybody deserves a
birthday." The car veers smoothly
to the right, loops the turn, and rolls
onto two lanes. The red sphere changes colors.
The cars swing from one lane to the other
as if drivers are handing off partners in a square dance.
We each move slowly now. I behind
the other, behind another, behind others,
making time as far as I can see.

CHANGE

If I could only tell you
what I think when you say,
"Change is good," I would
not become the cuttlefish,
camouflage myself with color,
and comb my hair back to the part
in platitudes. These words pierce
the work I bury myself under
to hide from the sharks
who can shear off my head
with a burn that I want to forget.
I want to tell the world
that this change has brought about
the destruction of a community
that has me carrying an abundance
of ink to fight off the casual chatter
of my enemies who frequent this floor
looking for my hidden door.

CHAIN OF EVENTS

The shadows from the trees deepened
along the street as the sun slipped
behind the trees, signaling the loss
of connection to the lives revealed daily
and shared in snippets on the job with coworkers.
The cars rolled out of the parking lot,
setting into motion separate yet tangled
chains of events. One car turned left out
of the parking lot; another rolled west and turned
left to go south. At the stop sign, a third car
pulled up beside the other to go left to north,
then east. Already immersed in separate worlds,
drivers faced straight ahead. All now
strangers rolling out to go left, then right.
The five o'clock day ended exhausted and
the streets busy as the cars separated
to roll away in different directions, to
realities more than those revealed daily.

WITH THE TOSS OF GLOVED HAND

Unaware,
the tossed aluminum can,
stripped of its wrapper, hit
the watery universe on its side.
It flipped bottom down,
top filling with swarming, swirling liquid
slapping over its rim
and pushing off in ripples.
The can gulped once,
choked and drowned,
before recycle.

LIFE ALONG THE HYPOTHETICAL

Along the cityscapes of cyberhighways,
hidden, punctilious pods of primed engines,

gambol at beckoning by nimble gloves and wired goggles
to mine the nuggets of thought, to divine
megabytes from judgment, opinion, and belief,

facsimiles strewn along the highway,
characters and symbols spawned by cookies and click streams
of behavior like abandoned styrene cups and broken bottle tops.

From dark cybernetworks to lonely cross borders,
among the cyberclouds to real-time chats, simple forays
Google into darkest thickets of midnight

to strip-mine innocence and elegance from content,
uncover hideaways of round robin,
pound strengths and foibles into virtual data stones.

Living there along the cyberhighway
in the clouds, data brokers sift and shift
human presence into gigabytes.

(Previously published in *Black & Rouge Review* 3, no. 1, Spring 2010)

AN URGE

I found a convention
of fuzz under my chair
huddled along the fifty-yard line
of a twelve-by-twelve-inch
vinyl floor square.

Waiting for the quarterback call,
what is it that fakes the curious?
The wind?
The cat?
The quarterback?

In a snap,
I noted that one
diagonally rolled back,
signaling immediately
a scrambling
of them all.

What is it—
this urge, this dare
to peek under a bed
or look under a chair?

(Previously published as "Discovery" in *Black & Rouge Review* 1, no. 1,
Spring 2008)

JEANS OR OTHER SUCH NO-NOS

If
it
is
inappropriate
to break
a rule,
why
does paying
to break it
make it right?

If
it
is
inappropriate
on Monday
but okay
on Friday
for money,
why
aren't
we
hypocrites?

HNT

It
was
jst
a
hnt
untl
then
it
happnd
      and
      I
      wonderd.
A
blnk
fast,
a
pause
but
slower,
      and
      I
      wonderd,
Hve
I
found
what
Im
looking
for?
      and
      I
      smiled.
Got it!

WHEN OLD MEMORIES COME TO VISIT

When old memories
come to find us,
they first trickle deep
from within the folds.
Then in wavy swirls,
like starlings spring
from their source.
The years train them
into thin threads
that cascade like spiderwebs,
loose and fragile, floating,
unattached in dance
in the regenerative partnership
between ourselves and our fantasies.

SIMPLE THINGS

Mesmerized by rhythmic swishing
of the murmuring dishwasher,
a blues drummer setting up
tempo for stance, water splaying
to the whistle of rotary sprinkler heads,
I am bathed in comfort tonight, wrapped
in the warm body of my robe, relaxing
with weight from the furry bundle on my chest,
in rhythmic swing of the hammock,
in yesteryears in June as cares float,
in and out on soft breezes from the past.
It is the simple things, it's true,
that sweep the heart up
and bring comfort in a sip of
smooth Chablis, a rye green pasture
in midday sunlight crowded by tall, lanky pines
tussling in the breezes for first place,
a row of visiting buttercups in early spring
resting against a plank fence on the North Forty.

SETTLING

Instead of warm, scrumptious
chocolate cake that forms a cradle
for melted chocolate topped with ice cream,
it was cold and hard.

That we settle for less at lunch and at life
and *what* we settle for is as much a part of the human condition
as the memory of water that sends the stream
downward
      in search
            of its lowest level.
               The domains
of difference and of distance lie
        between
that we want and *what* we want
in breakfast, in lovers, in careers;

that we expect and *what* we expect
along the distance between the seam
of the horizon and the edge of space.

Less than we think we are in others' eyes,
beads of truth strung on a chain of hard irony,
a mirror to the gap between the ends and the edges
of mind and heaven, of body and moon,
simultaneously revealing
that we are and *what* we are.

Printed in the United States
By Bookmasters